Dear Suzanne,

May you be inspired each day by the wisdom and beauty within these pages. Thank you for your gracious Southern hospitality —

With love,
Catherine

LOVE & PEACE

ALEXANDRA VILLARD
DE BORCHGRAVE

First published in 2020 by
GILES
An imprint of D Giles Limited
66 High Street, Lewes, BN7 1XG, UK
gilesltd.com

Creative Direction: Alexandra Villard de Borchgrave
Design: Henrique Siblesz, enlinea design
Photography of Illumination: Colleen Dugan, Freer|Sackler, Smithsonian Institution

Printed and bound in China

10 9 8 7 6 5 4 3 2 1

British Library Cataloging-in-Publication Data
De Borchgrave, Alexandra Villard.
Love & Peace: 37 Eternal Reflections
Alexandra Villard de Borchgrave;
—1st ed.
A catalogue record for this book is available from the British Library

ISBN: 978-1-911282-58-7

FOR ARNAUD

"Most precious adored wifey, As love grows old,
our own is deep, burning and unquenchable,
forever and ever —and beyond."

~ Arnaud de Borchgrave

"My Beloved, You are an integral part of my soul.
Your adoring wifey, in this world and the next."

~ Alexandra de Borchgrave

"who loves you, love him more..."
~ Sidi Abderrahman el Mejdub (1506–1568)

ETERNAL LOVE AND PEACE

While some are ready to die upon receiving a hopeless diagnosis, my beloved husband, Arnaud, was not. After confirmation of an incurable cancer, he would sit next to me, and say, "I don't want to leave you." In his typically brave style, Arnaud was ready to suffer whatever was necessary to fight for more time. We were defeated at every turn in seeking treatment, until one day he wistfully declared, "Someone up there wants me." I lay down beside him, enfolding him in my arms as the tears fell silently down my cheeks, knowing our 47 years of unbreakable love were drawing to a close. Yet deep within me, I found myself clinging to the faith that our story would not end here, that we were inextricably linked in life and in death.

Our journey together towards Arnaud's death began with a prayer two years before he fell ill. As he was in his eighties, I wished for more of a religious presence in our lives. One day I received a surprising email, the first indication of an answer to my prayer. It was from a Brother Gabriel from the Dominican House of Studies in DC. He wrote that he had received a copy of my book *Heavenly Order* and wanted to invite me to Evening Prayers in their chapel and supper in their refectory. Arnaud immediately exclaimed, "I'm coming with you."

Brother Gabriel and his friend, Brother Innocent, met us inside the chapel. Glowing in the setting sun that streamed through the windows was an exquisite gold Madonna from Belgium. My heart felt that this was another response to my prayer since Arnaud was born Belgian. Over supper, Arnaud astutely understood the true meaning of this contact, and with his marvelous jokes and tales, turned the encounter into the making of a special friendship.

In Arnaud's last months I would invite the Brothers to tea. Their spiritual reflections, steeped in the teachings of Saint Dominic, of the power of learning and worldly deprivation, were immensely consoling to us both.

At the moment of Arnaud's death, the Brothers blessed him with, "Godspeed Arnaud." Shortly thereafter, as if perfectly timed, the Brothers were ordained and sent to new parishes. They had entered our lives in our time of need like two angels and left, their mission of comfort completed.

Arnaud had promised he would do his best to send me a sign to prove the spirit lives on. That first night on my own, a kind friend said, "You must play some music so you won't feel so alone." As I got into bed and put out all the lights, I turned on a random music system. I was stunned to hear "It's Time to Say Goodbye" in Andrea Bocelli's beautiful voice. Surely, I sensed, Arnaud had chosen that song.

Six months later, he sent me a more sensational sign. A dear friend invited me to the theatre. Before leaving, I was sitting at my desk with the chair turned sideways to watch the news. Arnaud loved to hand out one-line joke cards to make everyone laugh, and I had kept a favorite card on my desk next to his photograph as a precious reminder of his unique sense of humor.

The emotive performance had me return home with profound sadness. As I entered my bedroom, the chair was as I had left it, but I saw with a shock that the little joke card, that had been sitting at the back of my desk, was now neatly placed in the center of the seat. I knew immediately Arnaud had put it there to cheer me up. He reassured me we were still connected and understood all that I was experiencing. I was filled with a sense of peace and felt comforted beyond measure. I kissed the card and put it back by his photograph.

To me, these remarkable signs from Arnaud are confirmation that our spirit continues on, and that love transcends all boundaries into eternity.

As Madame de Staël penned so eloquently in 1807, "Love is the emblem of eternity; it confounds all notion of time, effaces all memory of a beginning, all fear of an end..."

~ Alexandra Villard de Borchgrave

PROLOGUE

Let your love flow outward
through the universe,
To its height, its depth,
its broad extent,
A limitless love,
without hatred or enmity.
~ Lord Buddha

LOVE

Love is the emblem of eternity;
it confounds all notion of time;
effaces all memory of a beginning,
all fear of an end…

~ Germaine de Staël

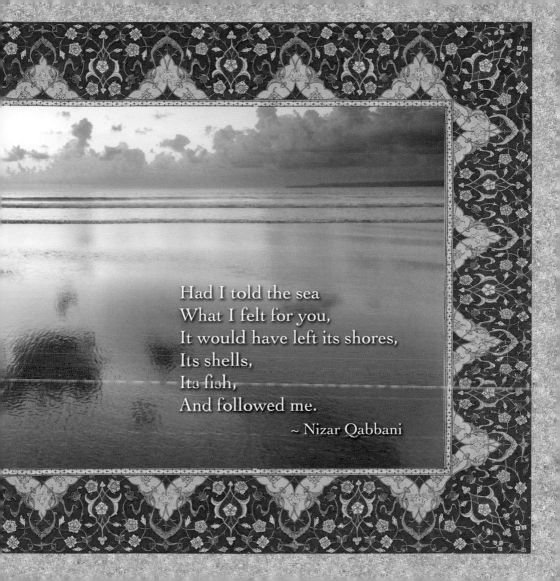

Had I told the sea
What I felt for you,
It would have left its shores,
Its shells,
Its fish,
And followed me.

~ Nizar Qabbani

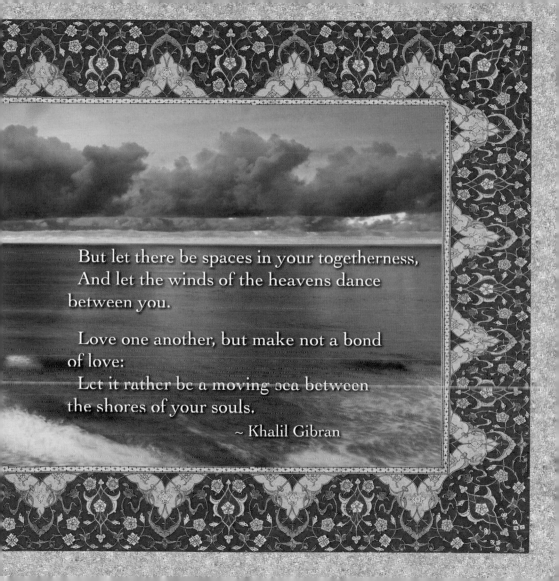

But let there be spaces in your togetherness,
And let the winds of the heavens dance
between you.

Love one another, but make not a bond
of love:
Let it rather be a moving sea between
the shores of your souls.

~ Khalil Gibran

I hope that real love and truth
are stronger in the end
than any evil or misfortune
in the world.

~ Charles Dickens

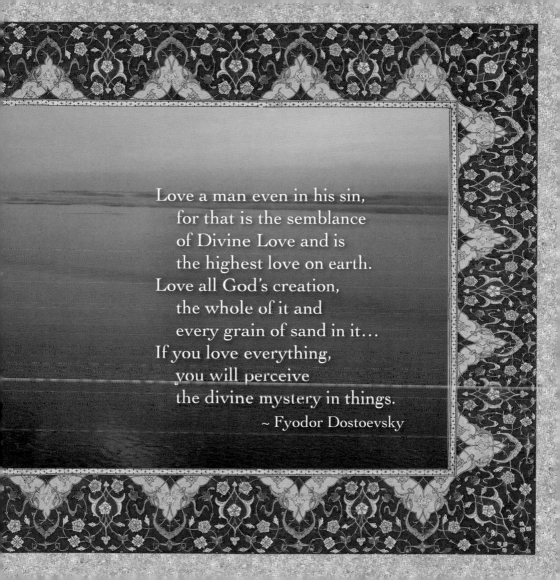

Love a man even in his sin,
for that is the semblance
of Divine Love and is
the highest love on earth.
Love all God's creation,
the whole of it and
every grain of sand in it…
If you love everything,
you will perceive
the divine mystery in things.

~ Fyodor Dostoevsky

JOY

Stay in the joy of now...
That center is a flowing spring,
a love and clarity.

~ Rumi

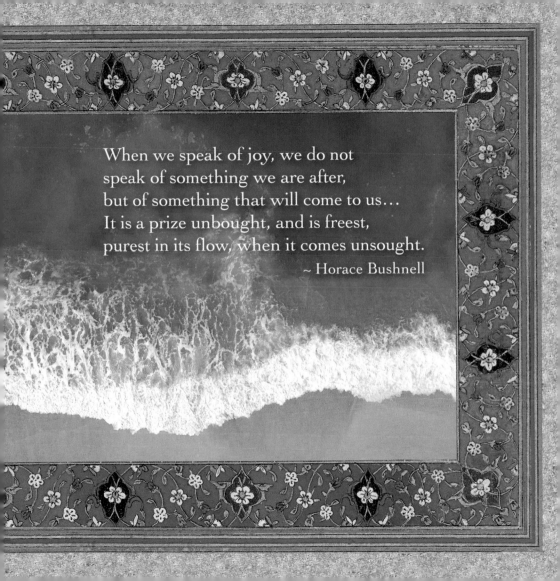

When we speak of joy, we do not
speak of something we are after,
but of something that will come to us…
It is a prize unbought, and is freest,
purest in its flow, when it comes unsought.

~ Horace Bushnell

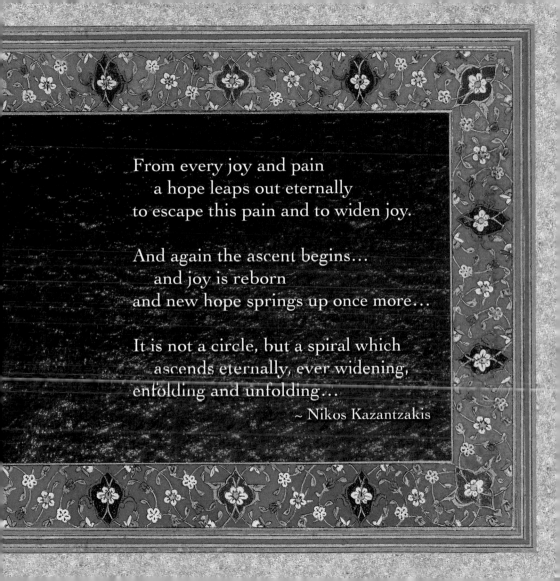

From every joy and pain
   a hope leaps out eternally
to escape this pain and to widen joy.

And again the ascent begins…
   and joy is reborn
and new hope springs up once more…

It is not a circle, but a spiral which
   ascends eternally, ever widening,
enfolding and unfolding…

~ Nikos Kazantzakis

Love is the ultimate meaning of everything around us. It is not a mere sentiment; it is truth; it is the joy that is at the root of all creation.
~ Rabindranath Tagore

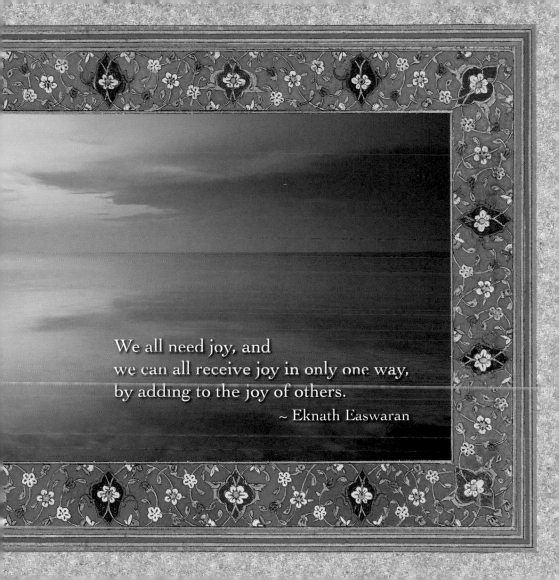

We all need joy, and
we can all receive joy in only one way,
by adding to the joy of others.

~ Eknath Easwaran

GRIEF

There is no sorrow beyond
the power of time…
~ Servius Sulpicius Rufus
to Cicero

There is a sacredness in tears.
They are not the mark of weakness,
    but of power.
They speak more eloquently
    than ten thousand tongues.
They are the messengers of
    overwhelming grief,
    of deep contrition,
    and of unspeakable love.

~ Washington Irving

Those who do not weep,
do not see.

~ Victor Hugo

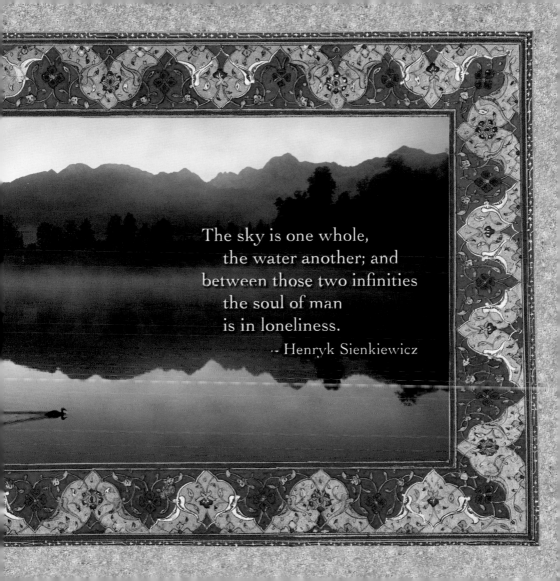

The sky is one whole,
the water another; and
between those two infinities
the soul of man
is in loneliness.
-- Henryk Sienkiewicz

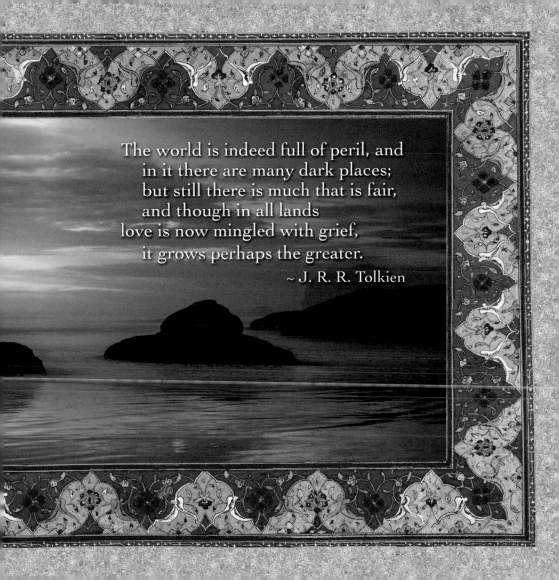

The world is indeed full of peril, and
in it there are many dark places;
but still there is much that is fair,
and though in all lands
love is now mingled with grief,
it grows perhaps the greater.

~ J. R. R. Tolkien

RESILIENCE

We shall draw from
the heart of suffering itself
the means of
inspiration and survival.
~ Sir Winston Churchill

The struggle is great, the task divine —
to gain mastery, freedom,
happiness, and tranquility.

~ Epictetus

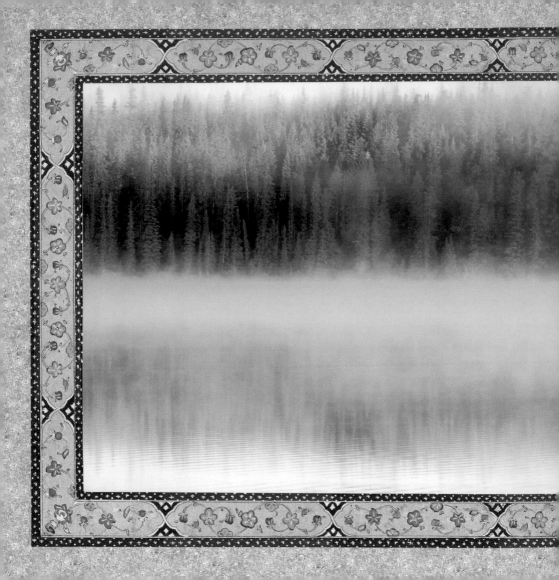

Endurance is the crowning quality,
and patience all the passion of great hearts...
~ James Russell Lowell

The work an unknown good man
has done is like a vein of water
flowing hidden underground,
secretly making the ground green.

~ Thomas Carlyle

The best and most beautiful things
in the world cannot be seen nor even
touched, but just felt in the heart.
~ Anne Sullivan

GRATITUDE

O Lord, that lends me life,
Lend me a heart
    replete with thankfulness!
        ~ William Shakespeare

Often, too, our own light goes out, and is rekindled by some experience we go through with a fellow-man. Thus we have each of us cause to think with deep gratitude of those who have lighted the flames within us.

~ Albert Schweitzer

To see a World in a Grain of Sand,
And a Heaven in a Wild Flower,
Hold Infinity in the palm of your hand,
And Eternity in an hour.

~ William Blake

We must love them both,
those whose opinions we share
    and those whose opinions we reject,
for both have labored
    in the search for truth,
and both have helped us in finding it.

-- Saint Thomas Aquinas

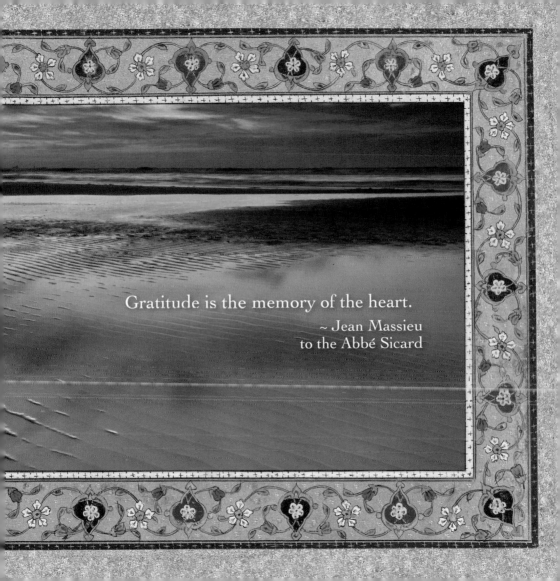

Gratitude is the memory of the heart.

~ Jean Massieu
to the Abbé Sicard

ENLIGHTENMENT

The sun is invisible in men,
but visible in the world,
yet both are of one
and the same sun.

~ Gerhard Dorn

Truth alone will endure,
all the rest will be swept
away before the tide of time.

~ Mahatma Gandhi

To a wise man, the whole earth is open; for the native land of a good soul is the whole earth.

~ Democritus

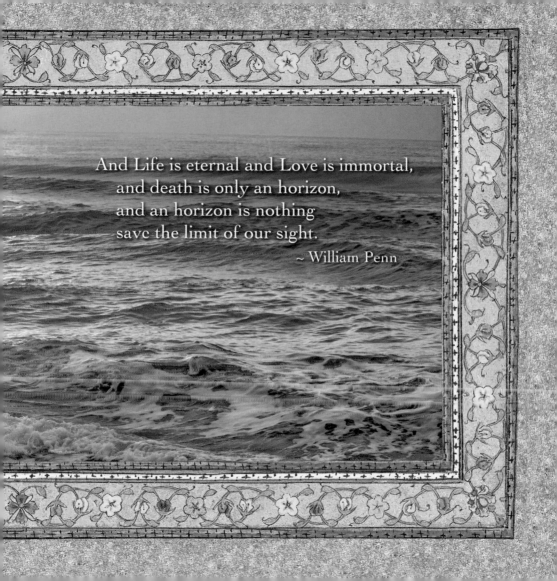

And Life is eternal and Love is immortal,
and death is only an horizon,
and an horizon is nothing
save the limit of our sight.

~ William Penn

For sometimes
it is an act of bravery
even to live.
~ Lucius Annaeus Seneca the Younger

PEACE

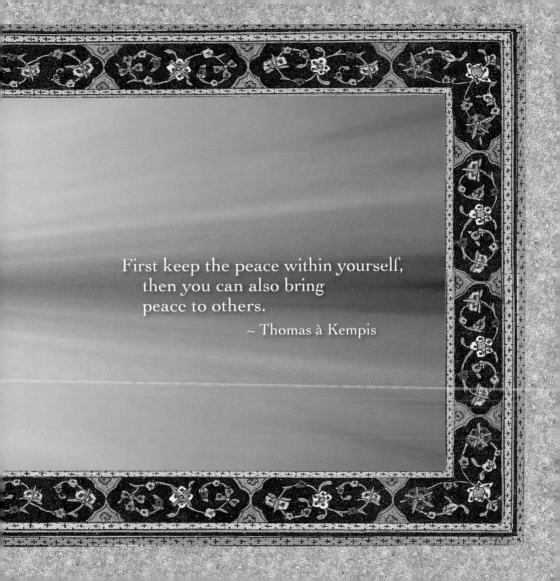

First keep the peace within yourself,
then you can also bring
peace to others.

~ Thomas à Kempis

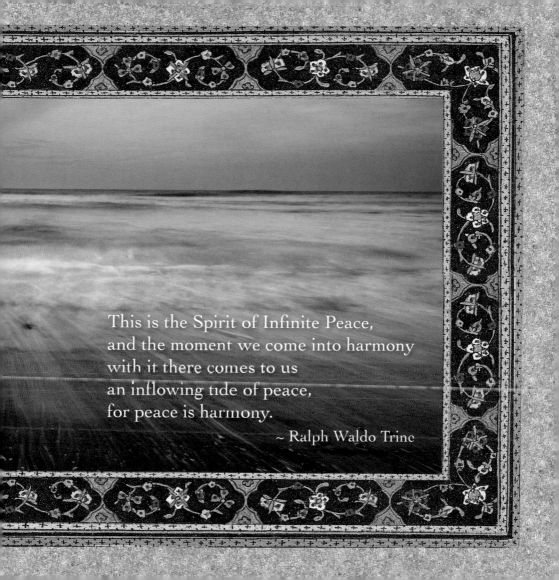

This is the Spirit of Infinite Peace,
and the moment we come into harmony
with it there comes to us
an inflowing tide of peace,
for peace is harmony.

~ Ralph Waldo Trine

Socrates: … grant that I may become beautiful within, and that whatever outward things I may have be in harmony with the spirit inside me.

~ Plato

Peace and love are ever in us,
being and working;
but we be not always in
peace and in love.

~ Julian of Norwich

Deep peace of the running wave to you.
Deep peace of the flowing air to you.
Deep peace of the quiet earth to you.
Deep peace of the shining stars to you.
Deep peace of the gentle night to you.

~ John Rutter
A Gaelic Blessing

EPILOGUE

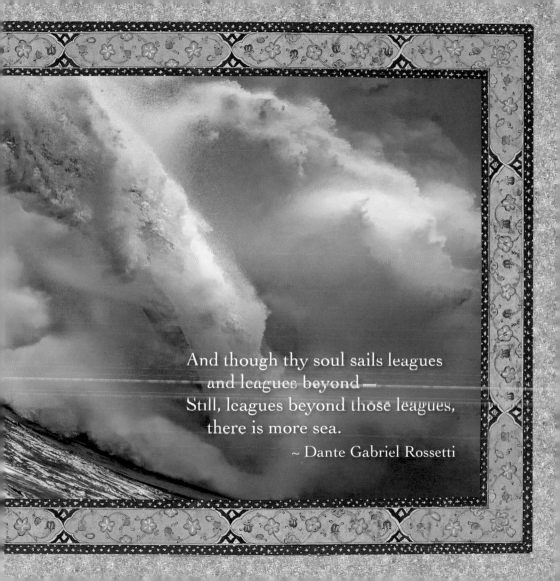

And though thy soul sails leagues
and leagues beyond —
Still, leagues beyond those leagues,
there is more sea.

~ Dante Gabriel Rossetti

INSPIRATION

We find inspiration from words, no matter when they were composed.

SAINT THOMAS AQUINAS
225–1274 · Italian
Dominican friar and prolific writer who combined the theological principles of faith with the philosophical principles of reason in the tradition of scholasticism. Known as the Doctor Angelicus and the Doctor Communis. Regent master in theology at the University of Paris *Summa Theologiae* c. 1265–1274.

WILLIAM BLAKE
1757–1827 · English
Poet and artist. Held in high regard by later critics for his expressiveness and creativity, and for the philosophical and mystical undercurrents within his work. *Fragments from Auguries of Innocence* written 1803, published 1863.

LORD BUDDHA
c. 563/480 BCE–c. 483/400
Founder of Buddhism and teacher in the pursuit of wisdom. From *Passage Meditation* by Eknath Easwaran, founder of the Blue Mountain Center of Meditation, copyright 2008; reprinted by permission of Nilgiri Press, P.O. Box 256, Tomales, CA 94971, www.bmcm.org.

HORACE BUSHNELL
1802–1876 · American
Congregational minister and theologian. Literary editor of the New York Journal of Commerce, and became a tutor at Yale. Josiah Hotchkiss Gilbert, *Dictionary of Burning Words of Brilliant Writers*, 1895.

THOMAS CARLYLE
1795–1881 · British
Historian, mathematician, and essayist born in Scotland whose most famous work was *The French Revolution*. *Dictionary of Quotations*, compiled by Rev. James Wood, 1899.

SIR WINSTON CHURCHILL
1874–1965 · British
British statesman, army officer, and writer who was Prime Minister of the United Kingdom from 1940–1945 and 1951–1955. *Sir Winston Churchill: A Self Portrait.* London: Eyre & Spottiswoode, 1954.

DEMOCRITUS
c. 460–c. 370 BC · Greek
Philosopher primarily known for his formulation of an atomic theory of the universe. Translation by Kathleen Freeman *Ancilla to the Pre-Socratic Philosophers: A Complete Translation to the Fragments in Diels, Fragmente der Vorsokratiker*, Reprinted by permission of Wiley-Blackwell, 1966.

GERMAINE DE STAËL
1766–1817 · French
Woman of letters and historian of Genevan origin whose lifetime overlapped with the events of the French Revolution and the Napoleonic era. Known as Madame de Stael. *Corinne*, 1807, as translated by Isabel Hill, 1833.

CHARLES DICKENS
1812–1870 · English
Writer and social critic. Creator of some of the most cherished fictional characters and acclaimed as the best novelist of his time. *David Copperfield*, 1850.

GERHARD DORN
1530–1584 · Belgian
Philosopher, translator, alchemist, and physician. *Theatrum Chemicum Volume 1 Spec.*

FYODOR DOSTOEVSKY
1821–1881 · Russian
Novelist, short story writer, essayist, journalist and philosopher. *The Brothers Karamazov*, 1879 1880 Book VI

EKNATH EASWARAN
1910–1999 · Indian
Spiritual teacher and author who developed the Passage Meditation method of meditation. From *The End of Sorrow* by Eknath Easwaran, founder of the Blue Mountain Center of Meditation, copyright 1975; reprinted by permission of Nilgiri Press, P.O. Box 256, Tomales, CA 94971, www.bmcm.org.

EPICTETUS
c. 55–c. 135 · Greek
Stoic philosopher born a slave in Rome, freed after Nero's death, who taught dispassionate acceptance of external events beyond control.

MAHATMA GANDHI
1869–1948 · Indian
Philosopher-Activist who led the Indian Independence movement against British Colonial rule. He believed in nonviolence and is known as the Father of the Nation. Posthumous publication *Basic Education*, 1951. Copyright permission from Navajivan Trust.

KHALIL GIBRAN
1883–1931 · Lebanese
Lebanese-American writer, poet, visual artist, and Lebanese nationalist. On Marriage — *The Prophet* A Borzoi Book, 1923.

VICTOR HUGO
1802–1885 · French
Poet, novelist, and dramatist of the Romantic movement. Regarded as one of the most brilliant and renowned French authors. *Les Misérables*, 1862.

WASHINGTON IRVING
1783–1859 · American
Acclaimed short story writer, biographer, historian, and Ambassador to Spain. The Reverend James Wood, comp. *Dictionary of Quotations*, 1899.

NIKOS KAZANTZAKIS
1883–1957 · Greek
Greek writer nominated for the Nobel Peace Prize. From THE SAVIORS OF GOD by Nikos Kazantzakis. Translation with intro by Kimon Friar. Copyright © 1960 by Helen Kazantzakis. Copyright renewed 1988 by Simon & Schuster, Inc. Reprinted with the permission of Simon & Schuster, Inc. All rights reserved. Global rights courtesy of © Niki Stavrou.

THOMAS À KEMPIS
1380–1471 · German-Dutch
Member of the Modern Devotion, a spiritual movement during the late medieval period. *The Imitation of Christ* c.1420.

JAMES RUSSELL LOWELL
1819–1891 · American
Romantic poet, critic, editor, and diplomat. *Columbus*, 1844.

JEAN MASSIEU
1772–1846 · French
A pioneering deaf educator who helped develop the first formalized French Sign Language. From a letter to the Abbé Sicard.

SIDI ABDERRAHMAN EL MEJDUB
1506–1568 · Moroccan
North African poet, Sufi, and mystic. *Outside & Subterranean Poems, a Mini-Anthology in Progress (56): Some Quatrains from Sidi Abderrahman el Mejdub (Al Jadida, early 16C.–Meknes 1568)* Translation from Arabic by Abdelfetah Chenni & Pierre Joris.

JULIAN OF NORWICH
1342–1416 · English
Ascetic of the Middle Ages who wrote the first surviving book in the English language to be written by a woman. *XVI Revelations of Divine Love*, 1670.

WILLIAM PENN
1644–1718 · English
Nobleman, writer, Quaker, advocate of religious freedom, and founder of the American Commonwealth of Pennsylvania. Prayer by William Penn.

PLATO
428–348BCE · Greek
Athenian philosopher in Ancient Greece, student of Socrates, teacher of Aristotle, founder of the Platonist school of thought, and the Academy, the first institution of higher learning. Republished with permission of Princeton University Press, from *The collected dialogues of Plato, including the letters* (Conclusion to the *Phaedrus*), Plato, 1961; permission conveyed through Copyright Clearance Center, Inc.

NIZAR QABBANI
1923–1998 · Syrian
Diplomat, poet, and publisher. His poetic style was simple and elegant, combining themes of love, eroticism, feminism, and religion. From *Arabian Love Poems*, by Nizar Kabbani, translated by Bassam K. Frangieh and Clementina R. Brown. Copyright © 1999 by Bassam K. Frangieh and Clementina R. Brown. Used with permission of Lynne Rienner Publishers, Inc.

DANTE GABRIEL ROSSETTI
1828–1882 · British
Soulful poet, illustrator, medieval revivalist painter, and translator of Italian poetry. *House of Life, 73, The Choice—III*, 1881.

SERVIUS SULPICIUS RUFUS
106 BC–43 BC · Roman
Orator and jurist who was a student of rhetoric with Cicero and the father of the female poet Sulpicia. Made proconsul of Achea by Caesar in 43BC. Servius Sulpicius to Cicero. Letters. The Harvard Classics, 1909–1914.

JALĀL AD-DĪN MUHAMMAD RŪMĪ — KNOWN AS RUMI
1207–1273 · Persian
Muslim jurist, Islamic scholar, and Sufi mystic poet whose main purpose was union with the Beloved. His writings promoted tolerance, goodness, charity, and awareness through love. *The Essential Rumi*, Translated by Coleman Barks.

JOHN RUTTER
1945 · English
Composer, conductor, editor, arranger, and record producer, mainly of choral music. Words by William Sharp (1855–1905) adapted by John Rutter, © 1978 The Royal School of Church Music. Used with permission.

LUCIUS ANNAEUS SENECA THE YOUNGER
c. 5BC–65 AD · Roman
Stoic philosopher, dramatist, scientist, statesman, and Consul of the Roman Empire in 55. SENECA, VOL. V, translated by Richard M. Gummere, Loeb Classical Library Volume 76, Cambridge, Mass.: Harvard University Press, First published 1920. Loeb Classical Library ® is a registered trademark of the President and Fellows of Harvard College.

ALBERT SCHWEITZER
1875–1965 · Alsatian
Theologian, organist, writer, humanitarian, philosopher, and physician. Nobel Peace Laureate 1952 From *The Light Within Us*, Philosophical Library, New York, 1959.

WILLIAM SHAKESPEARE
1564–1616 · English
Poet, actor, and playwright considered the finest writer in the English language of plays, sonnets, and narrative poems. *Henry VI*, Part II, King Henry c. 1590–91.

HENRYK SIENKIEWICZ
1846–1916 · Polish
Journalist, novelist and Nobel Peace Laureate in 1905, best remembered for his historical novel *Quo Vadis*, 1896. *The Lighthouse Keeper*, 1882. Translated by Jeremiah Curtin – Monadnock Valley Press.

ANNE SULLIVAN
1866–1936 · American
Tutor to Helen Keller, author, political activist, and lecturer. She was the first deaf-blind person to earn a Bachelor of Arts degree. From *The Story of My Life* by Hellen Keller, 1905.

RABINDRANATH TAGORE
1861–1941 · Indian
Poet, musician, and artist. First non-European to win the Nobel Peace Prize in Literature. *Sādhanā: The Realisation of Life*, 1916.

J.R.R. TOLKIEN
1892–1973 · English
Writer, poet, philologist, and academic. From *The Lord of the Rings*, *The Fellowship of the Ring*. Reprinted by permission of HarperCollins Publishers Ltd. © Tolkien, 1954.

RALPH WALDO TRINE
1866–1958 · American
Philosopher, author, and teacher of the new Thought Movement. *In Tune With The Infinite: Or, Fullness of Peace Power and Plenty*, 1897.

ENLIGHTENMENT
DIVIDER

Mathnavi heading folio (replacement) from the *Silsilat al-dhahab* (Chain of gold), first *daftar* (book) in the *Haft awrang* (Seven thrones) by Jami (d.1492). Purchase — Charles Lang Freer Endowment F1946.12.1

BORDER

Folio from a *Haft awrang* (Seven thrones) by Jami (d. 1492). Purchase — Charles Lang Freer Endowment F1946.12.140

IMAGES

MoreISO/Getty Images
apomares/Getty Images
Nopparat Thanatawan/Dreamstime
Nopparat Thanatawan/Dreamstime
AleksandarGeorgiev/Getty Images

PEACE
DIVIDER

Folio from a Qur'an, sura 114:1-6, left-hand half of a double-page finispiece. Purchase — Smithsonian Unrestricted Trust Funds, Smithsonian Collections Acquisition Program, and Dr. Arthur M. Sackler S1986.86.2

BORDER

Anthology. Purchase — Charles Lang Freer Endowment F1937.35a-b

IMAGES

macbrianmun/Getty Images
Design Pics Inc/National Geographic Creative
Design Pics Inc/National Geographic Creative
Remedios/Getty Images
Eric Gevaert/Dreamstime

EPILOGUE
IMAGE

JNEphotos/Getty Images

AUTHOR BIO
IMAGE

Tony Powell

ACKNOWLEDGMENTS

In this increasingly turbulent world, the beauty offered by the Freer Gallery of Art and the Arthur M. Sackler Gallery at the Smithsonian Institution creates an oasis of peace. I am deeply grateful for the opportunity to illustrate the messages in *Love & Peace: 37 Eternal Reflections* with their exquisite collection of sixteenth century Illumination manuscripts. I would especially like to thank Chase F. Robinson, Director; Massumeh Farhad, Chief Curator; Marjan Adib, Chief of Staff; Elisa Glazer, Director of Development; Colleen Dugan, museum photographer; and Jeffrey P. Cunard, Board of Trustees; for their gracious support.

Water became my inspiration for *Love & Peace*. As in *Love & Wisdom*, I chose wise reflections that have flowed through the tides of time to calm the spirit and bring us comfort. I cannot express enough gratitude to my distinguished publisher Dan Giles and his wonderful team for their efforts in making these books of hope a reality.

I could not have created this sequel without the extraordinarily creative skills of Henrique Siblesz. For over twelve years, Henri has helped me with his fine touch to realize my dream of bringing hope and healing to those who are suffering, and I thank him here with all my heart for his dedication to this mission of comfort.

My heartfelt thanks to my dear family and friends who have seen me through my seventh book, and to all those who have generously supported the Light of Healing Hope Foundation and made it possible for us to reach patients and their families suffering the adversity of life.

~ Alexandra Villard de Borchgrave

Water is essential to life and is one of the four elements that have defined our existence. Symbolic of purity, water can offer comfort and soothe us in times of need. The 37 eternal reflections in this book offer inspiration and are arranged through chapters in color associations.

LOVE	PINK
JOY	CYAN
GRIEF	VIOLET
RESILIENCE	GREEN
GRATITUDE	ORANGE
ENLIGHTENMENT	GOLD
PEACE	BLUE

© TONY POWELL

Alexandra Villard de Borchgrave has seven books to her credit and has built a reputation as an author, poet, photojournalist, and philanthropist. Her photographs have appeared on the covers of internationally renowned publications, such as *Newsweek* and *Paris Match*.

She is the co-author of *Villard: The Life and Times of an American Titan* (Nan A. Talese/Doubleday), a biography of her great-grandfather, railroad magnate and financier Henry Villard, who masterminded the creation of General Electric. Alexandra is the author of *Healing Light, Heavenly Order,* and *Beloved Spirit* (Glitterati Inc.); *To Catch A Thought* (Light of Healing Hope Foundation); and *Love & Wisdom* (D Giles Ltd.).

Based in Washington DC, Mrs. de Borchgrave founded the Light of Healing Hope Foundation, a 501(c)(3) non-profit organization, in 2010 with the mission of giving books as gifts to hospitals and hospices to bring comfort and healing to those in need.